SISTER MARIETTA
✠
SAGINAW'S SAINT

SISTER MARIETTA

✠

SAGINAW'S SAINT

Joan & Craig Douglas

SISTER MARIETTA, SAGINAW'S SAINT

Published by
Emmaus House of Saginaw, 501 (c) 3
733 S. 14th Street
Saginaw, Michigan 48601
www.emmaushousesaginaw.com

Printed in the United States of America

First Edition: January 2021

Book cover and interior layout design by Vickie Swisher, Studio 20|20, with prior assistance from Mark Myczkowiak, retired editor/publisher of *The Catholic Weekly*, Carrollton, Michigan

Printed by Color House Graphics, www.colorhousegraphics.com

ISBN 978-1-7363941-0-6 (softcover)

This book is dedicated to Bill Schaefer
and
the thousands of faithful volunteers like Bill
who have kept Emmaus House viable for thirty-three years.
Bill Schaefer was a retired engineer who came three days a
week for years to keep Emmaus House in good repair.
His greatest gift, however, was himself, a beautiful role model
of a man for the Emmaus women, many of whom
had never known such a good and caring man.

– Sr. Marietta Fritz, December 15, 2019

TABLE OF CONTENTS

Introduction ix

Chapter 1: Take the First Step 1

Chapter 2: The Other Poor 3

Chapter 3: The Voice of Warnella Humphrey 5

Chapter 4: Dad's Daughter 7

Chapter 5: Each House: A Home 9

Chapter 6: "Coping" 11

Chapter 7: Humble 13

Chapter 8: The Questions 15

Chapter 9: Hell 17

Chapter 10: The Tragedies 19

Chapter 11: Kind 21

Chapter 12: Resiliency 23

Chapter 13: What Can Be Funny? 25

Chapter 14: Weeding the Garden 27

Chapter 15: A Day in the Life 29

Chapter 16: Believing in Others 33

Memories Intermission 35

Chapter 17: A Transformation 49

Chapter 18: The Guests 51

Chapter 19: "Love" 59

Chapter 20: A New Role 61

Chapter 21: Taking the Reigns 65

Chapter 22: A Time to Perform 67

Chapter 23: Enter Donna 71

Chapter 24: Donna's Story 73

Chapter 25: Takila's Story 75

Chapter 26: Saginaw Leaders' Perspectives 77

Epilogue 83

The Authors 85

Donation Support 86

*"The two were going to a village named Emmaus…
and Jesus drew near and walked along with them."*

– LUKE 24:13-15

THIS BOOK IS ABOUT SISTER MARIETTA FRITZ and the dedication of her lifetime of work to help those in need.

Recognition should also be given to Sister Shirley Orand. A true risk taker, Sister Shirley is often referenced today as if she were still among us. But the truth is, Sister Shirley passed away in 1993, losing a hard fought battle with cancer. While she has not been here in an earthly sense since then, her presence is acknowledged and felt.

Starting with one home (labeled House One), the sisters expanded their mission of assisting troubled women as houses became available. As they were added, they were labeled by their number in the order of acquisition (e.g. House Two, House Three, and so on).

Sister Marietta has received many honors over the years for the work of Emmaus House, and, in each case, in her own humble way, she is quick to honor the memory of Sister Shirley.

Throughout her life, Sister Marietta seems to have "found" the poor, both monetarily and spiritually. In deciding to step forward and create the Emmaus House program, she was quite certain those poor in spirit who needed help would find her.

This became the driving force in her life:

"Help those who have less."

– *Joan Douglas*

SISTER MARIETTA APPROACHED THE YOUNG WOMAN WHO HAD JUST BEEN RELEASED FROM THE SAGINAW COUNTY JAIL. She introduced herself and explained that a part of her job as chaplain was to provide a ride to women when they were released, and there was no one at the jail to take them home.

The woman just stared at her. Sister repeated her offer. The ex-inmate kept looking beyond Sister and down the street. She began to walk away but turned back and said, "Someone will be around."

Sister knew what this response meant. She could see another likely revolving door of leaving jail, returning to the same circle on the street and the same crimes which caused her arrest. Sister knew her mission was made clear: shut the door.

"Blessed are the merciful; for they shall obtain mercy."
– MATTHEW 5:7

CHAPTER 1

Take the First Step

"*Love bears all things, hopes all things, believes all things, endures all things...love never fails.*"

— I CORINTHIANS 13:7-8

"*Take the first step in faith. You don't have to see the whole staircase, just take the first step.*"

— MARTIN LUTHER KING, JR.

THE EMMAUS HOUSE PROJECT BEGAN IN SEPTEMBER OF 1987 when Sister Marietta and Sister Shirley discussed the vision that both had to provide a safe place for women to go upon leaving jail, prison, or rehabilitation. They located a building, and believed miracles would occur there; they just didn't have any money.

The miracles began and boxes of donated items appeared on the porch. Volunteers came forward and donations (checks) started to arrive in the mail. It was happening. Support came from churches and individuals who had heard of this new ministry and believed in the Sisters' vision.

Word continued to spread and their goal to provide "guests" with not only the day to day essentials, but also guidance, therapy, a sense of community and a home, became real. "We really did start without a penny and that is amazing...that was a miracle", Sister Marietta said recently. "God had us start Emmaus House to save us and I hope we have helped a few others along the way", added Sister Shirley.

When she was a teenager, Sister Marietta's brother bet her $5.00 that she wouldn't enter the convent. She won that bet. Not certain where this path would take her, she told herself to be open and accept whatever responsibilities she would be given. Math teacher, cook, jail chaplain, and founder of Emmaus House, her journey has been filled with many rewards, love, heartache, frustration, and a lasting belief that her God traveled the road with her.

– *Joan Douglas*

CHAPTER 2

The Other Poor

*"Blessed are those who have regard for the weak;
the Lord will deliver them in times of trouble."*

– PSALMS 41:1

"WHY DO WE HAVE TO CUT THE NEIGHBOR'S LAWN?" Sister's father replied, "Because it needs cutting." Born into a farm family of seven children, Sister Marietta knew they were poor. Everything that could be saved, was. What they lacked in income, was made up for by an abundance of love and respect for each other. A passion to help others developed in Sister from an early age as she witnessed her parents lending a hand to anyone in need. "We were poor but didn't think of ourselves as poor, so we just helped the 'other poor'."

Often called upon to babysit, Sister helped a man who had lost his wife and needed help caring for his children while he was at work. Sister was thrilled when he paid her $5.00 and went home to share the story of her new wealth. Sister's mother explained to her that when someone needed your help, you did not take money. She returned the $5.00.

"Well done, good and faithful servant."

– MATTHEW 25:21

When Sister Marietta was seven years old, she had her first paper route. "I was tall for my age, so I think that is why I got jobs." She was also a frequent babysitter; she cleaned houses, and took in laundry. Sister would grow up to complete her undergraduate degree at Our Lady of Cincinnati College and her Masters Degree in mathematics from Notre Dame University and taught in Catholic schools for 18 years. Often given the students who struggled with academic concepts, Sister embraced them. She accepted the challenge, echoing again the forces of her childhood and the teachings of her parents. "Do a good job, and always do your best job."

Thus, she always stood by her beliefs. At one school, a first year teacher who was not a nun was fired in order to be replaced by a nun to, frankly, save money. When sister learned of the details of the situation and knew in her heart what this very fine teacher was going through, Sister quit. "I have always stood up for what I thought was right. That can, however, mean having to move from place to place."

Sister was then assigned to cook for her order for one year. While cooking was a mastered skill, this was a particularly challenging position, since she had struggled with an eating disorder throughout her life. Sister believed she needed to let those who made assignment decisions know that she felt called to work in a jail setting, believing her skills would be put to a greater good. That call came and Sister arrived in Saginaw.

– *Joan Douglas*

CHAPTER 3

The Voice of
Warnella Humphrey Wright

"I am the good shepherd, and I know my sheep."

– JOHN 10:14

"IN 1978, I MET A GOD-FILLED, LOVING WOMAN at the Saginaw County Jail. She had a smile that lit up the entire jail, and she had a heart of gold. Sister Marietta opened her heart to me and shared with me that God loved me, and I could do better. I never thought I could be a good person. She let me know that I was still a child of God, and God never leaves or gives up on his children. We leave Him. He still continues to remain there for us, with open arms.

Sister taught me so many things: how to pray and talk to God. I learned to crochet and knit. Sister prayed for me every day and for so many years and continues to pray to this day. This woman of

God gave from her heart, never judging. At times, she was stern, but, at the same time, giving me hope and showing me her love. There were no games that you could play on her; she was wise in all areas of behavior.

Sister Marietta helped me to see the light while I was in a dark place. She taught me to hold my head up high when the shame I felt kept me from feeling good. This woman helped me to walk straight, after I had been on the crooked path of destruction. The smile and the light in my heart that was gone, returned. She taught me to forgive myself.

And, Sister taught me to give to others. I needed to give my time, talents, hope, and strength from my heart and not for monetary gain, especially after all the taking I had done.

Sister is a woman of love, courage, strength, and faith and has devoted her life to make Emmaus a home, so that I and so many other women could learn to live happy and good lives.

From my heart to yours, I love you, Sister, and all that you have given me."

– *Warnella Humphrey Wright, Ex-guest of Emmaus House*

CHAPTER 4

Dad's Daughter

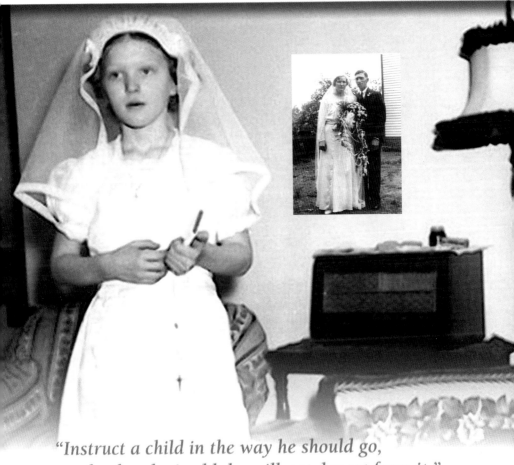

*"Instruct a child in the way he should go,
and, when he is old, he will not depart from it."*

– PROVERBS 22:6

SISTER ONCE SHARED THAT "I AM MY DAD'S DAUGHTER." Her father was spiritually driven, never seeking wealth. Early on, she believed she not only understood the way he lived his life, but also realized her world view was much the same. Sister believed that "So many earthly things don't matter because I am on a different kind of journey."

Sister's father set the example which helped define her. Sister had gotten to know an inmate named "Willie" in the Saginaw County Jail when she worked there as chaplain. She had shared stories with Willie regarding growing up poor in a farmer's family where the only abundant thing was love. Upon his release, Willie asked Sister if she would take him to her home in Cincinnati so that he could stay with her family and get a "clean start." Sister drove Willie to Cincinnati, and her father welcomed him in and treated him like a son.

And, so it was with him, a father mindful of others' needs, always reaching out to help anyone who needed help, and he had the gift of engaging anyone he met in friendly conversation. Sister's mother commented to him that if the Pope himself walked into their home, he would probably sit right down and begin a conversation. Her father replied, "Well we wouldn't just let him stand there."

– *Joan Douglas*

CHAPTER 5

Each House: A Home

*"Carry each other's burdens, and in this way,
you will fulfill the law of Christ."*

— GALATIANS 6:2

SINCE ONE HOUSE CAN ONLY HOLD A FINITE NUMBER OF GUESTS and the demand for a place to go to after release from prison, jail, or rehab continued to quickly rise, more homes were needed. The miracle continued.

The Rodarte Builders began donating houses while electricians, plumbers, and mechanics came forward to donate their time and skill to fix up the houses and make certain that everything was up to code. A system of assigning House Managers to each home went into place to guide the guests in keeping with established rules to sustain safe and clean living. The ladies had weekly schedules to follow which included completing household chores and yard work, sharing in meal preparation, and helping with work that was needed at Emmaus and the Morrow Center, sorting donations and keeping the center user friendly. Step up houses were established for those guests who had proven trustworthy and could live with less supervision.

Sister wanted each house to feel like a home; the ladies attended church services, group meetings (AA, NA), and looked forward to monthly dinners out at an agreed upon restaurant. Viewing the Fourth of July fireworks celebration, an annual picnic, and a special trip to Michigan Adventure also provided positive group experiences.

Holidays are very special. Christmas is a time of gifts for all the guests, their children and grandchildren. Ex-guests are also included, as well as board members and volunteers, and are invited to the holiday dinner and evening of songs and games. Each house is decorated with a Christmas tree, wreaths and ornamental items, donated over the years. It is a time of celebration and thankfulness to the Lord for the gifts of the past year and the hope for a new and blessed year ahead. Easter is another time of rejoicing and includes Easter baskets, and an Easter egg hunt, dinner together, and attending special services.

The guests of Emmaus know they are welcome to stay for as long as they feel they need this environment of support. Some remain for a relatively short time; others may stay a year or more. In all, over 3,000 guests have lived and received services from the Emmaus House.

At one time, the cash box was stolen from Emmaus House, and, ultimately, the guest, Donna, who had stolen it was brought to trial and sentenced. House managers did not want her back in the fold; after all, she had stolen from SISTER. However, Sister welcomed her back.

Since that time, "Donna" went from a step-up house to her own apartment and returns weekly to Emmaus to visit and volunteer. Sister explained that when an ex-guest needed to return, it was right to give her another chance. "God would welcome her back home."

– *Joan Douglas*

CHAPTER 6

"Coping"

"Truly I tell you, whatever you did for one
of the least of the brothers and sisters of mine,
you did for me."

— MATTHEW 25:40

"MOST OF THESE WOMEN ARE BEAUTIFUL PEOPLE who have
been abused so much that their beauty does not shine through." Sister
saw what the scars of sexual abuse, emotional neglect, hunger, the fear
of how to live through the day and stay warm, how these real demons
haunted the guests and haunted Sister. "Sometimes, I just want to
hold them and cry with them."

Sister shared that she had been asked more than once whether she was afraid that a guest or someone holding a grudge against a guest would kill her. She has experienced conflicts, outbursts of anger, threats, etc., but believes she has always been safe. Yet, she concedes, "If any one of the ladies killed me, well, this is the way I have chosen to live my life, to live with inmates. I would gladly die if I knew one of the ladies could get off the streets and be saved from her life."

The funerals are very difficult, but Sister thought it was important to attend every one, and she did. The children, siblings, relatives, and friends seldom attend. Death comes early for the majority of the guests. Of the over 3,000 guests who have stayed at Emmaus House, only one has lived to be more than 70 years old. That their suffering ends, brings some comfort, yet Sister believes each one deserves "the same kind of heaven I am banking upon...I could not be happy in heaven if I did not think my ladies would be there, also."

When Sister worked as a jail chaplain, an inmate, Diane, delivered a baby boy. She promised Sister that she would not try to keep him but would give him up to a family who could properly take care of him. When she was released, she did not pursue gaining custody of her son. A family was found, willing to adopt him. Diane returned to the streets. Sister did not see her again. She recalled how Diane had shared with her that she could remember stealing fruit when she was about eight years old for her and her family. Diane could not recall ever feeling loved or looked after. Sister had difficulty coping with Diane's tragic story, but her response was, "We just need to keep on picking up the pieces."

Sister prays for every guest and every House every day. She has seen two generations of guests come through the door, mother and then daughter. This is one of the harshest realities; knowing that the crimes and abuses a mother has gone through are transferred to her daughter.

Sister has always believed that if one asks for forgiveness and willingly serves the Lord, that He accepts all, no matter the background, nor the mistakes made. As she had so often said, it is up to each of us to "switch on the light and live in the light."

– *Joan Douglas*

CHAPTER 7

Humble

"I and my father are one."

WHEN I FIRST MET SISTER MARIETTA FRITZ IN 1998, I WAS
STRUCK BY HER HUMILITY. I had heard her speak at the "Bishop's
Breakfast" aptly named meeting of Saginaw area leaders organized by
the late Bishop Kenneth Untener. Bishop Untener introduced Sister
Marietta that morning, who spoke, without notes, for 20 minutes,
about the history of the Emmaus House of Saginaw before we had
breakfast. After eating Sister Marietta fielded questions for another
20 minutes about "her ladies" the female residents of Emmaus House
who had been incarcerated or rehabilitated.

Here we were, listening to Sister Marietta, a co-founder of the most unique residential center in the State. Sister captivated the audience, explaining how she and Sister Shirley started without funding, with literally no resources other than an unstoppable will to accomplish feats others like me would judge beyond reach.

Sister Marietta wore a clean, simple dress. Her appearance underscored an existence based upon hope, faith, and love. She spoke softly that morning, without a microphone. All of us heard her.

During breakfast, she made it a point to speak with each of us, showing respect for her audience. This is my first remembrance of Sister Marietta and how incredibly humble she is.

This was reinforced multiple times during 2013–2014 when I was a frequent volunteer at the Emmaus House. Joan and I would arrive at 8:30 a.m., typically on a Wednesday. Sister Marietta would be in her office, already having worked an hour or more. Bill Schaefer would be in the chair next to her, going over the needs of the residents and their homes. Bill Schaefer was one of the most intelligent and ingenious persons anyone could ever meet. Once I saw Bill take apart a dryer based upon what he had viewed on a "you tube" video at his computer the night before, in order to accomplish a repair. Bill would always defer to Sister Marietta, however, in questions of repairs. He did this because of the respect he had for her and her role in leading the Emmaus House. Yet, Sister Marietta never assumed a position of authority in this regard; in her humble way she would listen to Bill and defer to his wisdom while steering tasks to the most efficient, cost-effective paths.

Humble. Sister Marietta Fritz remained humble throughout. My theory is she saw herself – along with Joan and all the volunteers – as God's servants. "We need to let God do his work; He has a plan," she would say. Despite her successes and her honors, Sister Marietta Fritz remained humble.

– *Craig Douglas*

CHAPTER 8

The Questions

"For I, the Lord your God, hold your right hand;
it is I who say to you, 'Fear not,
I am the one who helps you'."

— ISAIAH 41:13

"SISTER, WILL I GO TO HELL?" an inmate asked Sister while she was working in the Saginaw County Jail. This question brought Sister to share her own theology. She believes that God does not "put" people in hell; those who have been in jail or prison for crimes committed are suffering here on earth. In turn, God sent his only son to suffer and die for our sins, and that we are forgiven. Would God want his children to suffer again in the after-life?

Sister was once asked about mass murderers. Surely they cannot expect to enter heaven. Sister replied "God is like electricity – he is in us, but we have to flip the switch to turn on the light; anyone can do that."

No matter where her assignment took her from serving the church, to teaching, cooking, and working with those in jail, she felt that she and God were one, together in this life's journey.

"A HOUSE OF MIRACLES"

When women reach Emmaus House, typically, they arrive totally devastated, no family support, no faith, no goals, no resources for living. Sister recalls, "We had to start from scratch to see what they needed to survive and how we could help them."

The many stories of women whose lives had been shattered through physical and emotional abuse, often at the hands of family members, became routine. One guest shared that at age 11 she began having sex for pay (her mother was a prostitute), using drugs, and skipping school. At 12, she left home, hooked up with others who promised they would help her and found herself homeless in Detroit. She arrived at Emmaus in her mid-forties, without a birth certificate or identification of any kind, and she had never had a job. She found a home.

Sister often asked herself what could possibly keep these women going, and she determined that there is a powerful force within us that, when unleashed, tells us we can "make it", even against gigantic odds.

Sister Shirley and Sister Marietta gave the guests that support which can lead to finding direction, liking one's self, setting and achieving goals. So that even for those who lost twenty years or more from their lives while in prison, they could make it, could complete a GED, enroll in college courses, find employment, and be empowered to live drug free lives. And, as trusting relationships developed among the ladies through group meetings, morning meditation, and shared stories, and experiences, Sister concluded, "They helped to save each other's lives."

– *Joan Douglas*

CHAPTER 9

Hell

*"He will punish those who do not know God
and do not obey the gospel of our Lord Jesus."*

– 2 THESSALONIANS 1:8

I HEARD SISTER TALK ABOUT THE EXISTENCE OF HELL IN THE CONTEXT THAT SHE DOES NOT BELIEVE IN ITS EXISTENCE. AT ALL!

Simply put, Sister Marietta describes hell as "not being in the Bible."

I am not a biblical scholar, but I have attended close to 2,000 church services as an adult (My rough calculation: 46 years as an adult, conservative average of 40 services per year, is an estimated 1,840 Sunday services). Frankly, I have not heard this from the pulpit ever before.

Can you imagine how this impacts her residents? For them to hear there is no hell after all? It sticks for them, too!

An absence of hell is a stunning revelation for them! To consider that their sins may be forgiven, that there is indeed, hope, and that they need not fear going to hell...well, it is a motivator for most if not all of the residents. For Sister to say this, she is also quick to admit that many of her residents have experienced hell here on earth. Sister Marietta shared her belief that up to 90% of her residents have lived the life of prostitution. Hell! Marietta also describes the hell that exists in prison and jail ("If we treated our animals like we do our prisoners we would all be thrown into jail," Sister often declared to Joan and me in conversation.)

Maybe that is why Sister was so clear in her belief. The hell here on earth was enough. God could not add to that hell by creating another place for people to suffer. Her God – our God – is a loving God and would not place His children in hell.

For Joan and me, this is a wonderful message. And we have not been imprisoned! Can one imagine how comforting the message is for women who have made harmful and illegal choices, and been sent away for long periods of time, a liberating message for persons who have been treated as they have been treated, having been shunned by family members and society at large!

Residents, who have been locked up with little hope for a large portion of their lives, to receive this message from Sister is a precious gift. To think about eternal life, with a loving Lord and Savior, is energizing!

– *Craig Douglas*

CHAPTER 10

The Tragedies

*"For the lamb at the center of the throne
will be their shepherd, he will lead them
to springs of living water, and God will
wipe away every tear from their eyes."*

– REVELATIONS 7:17

JOANNE DIED IN AN ABANDONED BUILDING by natural causes, untreated pneumonia. She had been beaten by her husband leaving a leg so badly broken that amputation was recommended. She later revealed to Sister that she had an abortion when she was much younger but could not forgive herself. She ultimately healed at Emmaus House but went back to the street.

Jeannie's first abortion occurred at age nine. She had been impregnated by her stepfather, and, at age 10, the process repeated itself. No family member or anyone else came forward to report. She ran away to the streets. Her mother remained with her stepfather. She was found 10 days after she left. Her stepfather told Jeannie that her mother had overdosed.

Tanya quit school at age 12. She could not stand the harassment coming from other students because she smelled so bad. Her mother did not buy soap; shampoo, new clothes, etc., because she no longer cared. She was both a drug and alcohol abuser before Tanya was born. Drug possession sent Tanya to prison.

These three examples could be multiplied many times over. Guests' lives sometimes end tragically. Yet, Sister's response clearly remained steadfast, "We just need to keep on picking up the pieces."

— Joan Douglas

CHAPTER 11

Kind

*"Ask, and it shall be given you;
seek, and ye shall find;
knock and it shall be opened unto you."*

– MATTHEW 7:7

SISTER MARIETTA FRITZ AND HER CO-FOUNDER, SISTER SHIRLEY ORAND, GREW THE EMMAUS HOUSE OF SAGINAW, starting with one home and a half dozen ladies out of jail, prison, or rehabilitation. Soon, the number of homes grew, each numbered in the order of acquisition. The year I volunteered, the numbers had ballooned to 13 homes and 50 residents.

It is hard to imagine all of the conversations in which Sister Marietta has engaged with the residents. Couple them with the interactions she has had with funders, board members, volunteers, and community leaders, one has to acknowledge Marietta's kind approach. Incredibly patient, Sister Marietta is a careful listener. Each resident realized how well Sister listened. Her eyes lock in and her head nods in agreement. This simple skill is so overlooked in society today, and because she "had it," it was clear this gave her a huge advantage when meeting with people.

A resident might stumble; these are the most difficult conversations. She may have run afoul of the law or one of Sister's rules. You can imagine it would be a significant personal disappointment to Sister; perhaps it is a resident for whom Sister Marietta had given funds. The transgression would set back the resident and perhaps risk money previously granted. Marietta always set aside her personal feelings and displayed an even keel, a level of kindness.

People would copy her, using her behavior as a model. When Sister Marietta would speak softly to a resident who was raising her voice, the voice would soften to match Sister's voice. Residents would hold doors open and speak, "Hello," or other greetings to each other. Whenever lead handyman Bill Schafer needed help with a task, volunteers would step forward. In short, Sister's kindness was infectious. It rubbed off on residents, volunteers, board members, and contributors. Kind. Being kind was a code of conduct and a way of life at the Emmaus House of Saginaw due to Sister Marietta Fritz.

– *Craig Douglas*

CHAPTER 12

Resiliency

"My flesh and my heart may fail, but God is the strength of my heart and my portion forever."

— PSALM 73:26

TO DATE, ONLY ONE GUEST HAS LIVED TO BE 70 YEARS OLD. The abuses suffered, the toll on their bodies, and the inability to have health problems addressed while incarcerated lead to severe, life-threatening situations. Yet, with over 3,000 guests housed at Emmaus, only six have committed suicide.

Debra's suicide remains impossible for Sister to forget. Severely mentally ill, abused from childhood, fearful to be "out there" away from the shelter of Emmaus House, Debra, at age 48, returned for the sixth time. "This time, Sister, I am going to make it."

She remained at Emmaus for several years. Debra was able to get a job, a car, and, eventually, an apartment in a senior citizens' complex. She was never able, however, to control her fears and frequently took herself to the hospital emergency unit, believing there was something wrong with her that had not been diagnosed. Ultimately, she decided to give up her fight to stay alive.

"Granny," as she referred to herself, came to Emmaus from prison at the age of 66. She did not have a family, had never had children, and, it appeared then, not a very bright future. She persevered. Granny stayed at Emmaus for two years. She received unconditional love and support which led to her success in living independently, a short distance from Emmaus on Perkins Street. Sister took her to mass each Sunday so Granny could worship with her. Granny remains in her house and worships each Sunday.

Sister Marietta has felt the deep frustration of watching guests lose their hope, their faith, and return to the streets; yet, others, like Granny, have beaten the odds. Sister often quoted another Sister (Theresa): "I am not called to be successful but to be faithful."

– *Joan Douglas*

CHAPTER 13

What Can Be Funny?

"Freely you have received, freely give."

– MATTHEW 10:8

IT WAS HOLLY'S TURN TO PREPARE THE EVENING MEAL. Holly was not fond of cooking but put together a breakfast theme and then realized there was no juice in the house. She decided it was okay to pray to God for orange juice since the weekly groceries had already been purchased.

Later that afternoon, 300 cases of Sunny Delight were delivered as a donation. Sister was pleased with Holly's story of answered prayer but gave her a smiling caution to "Only pray for what you need."

Evenings are often spent playing board games. Yahtzee is a favorite as well as working jigsaw puzzles. One evening, Jeremy was visiting his mother, a guest at Emmaus. He decided that Sister would be a good helper to put together the 1,000 piece puzzle he had selected. When Sister questioned his choice, thinking it was quite a task for one evening, he replied, "Doesn't God give you miracles, so wouldn't he help us do this?"

Many guests struggle with reading, and their backgrounds of moving around, missing school, or quitting contribute to this deficit. Thus, Sister decided to have them spend some time reading aloud to each other. While some of the mispronounced words brought forth smothered chuckles, some were so difficult to understand that a guest usually called out, "That's not even a word! Sorry." Sister continued this practice believing that the more they listened to each other, they became "women really helping women."

– Joan Douglas

CHAPTER 14

Weeding the Garden

"Bear with each other and forgive one another..."

– COLOSSIANS 3:13

DANTE, ONE OF THE GUESTS, BELIEVED THAT SHE HAD QUITE A GREEN THUMB and really enjoyed tending to the vegetable garden and keeping it "weed free." After experiencing the following episode, she would later admit she sometimes "confused some flowers with weeds."

On a warm summer morning, Dante set out to spruce up the flower beds surrounding the Morrow Center. There were many long weeds embedded in the lilies. She worked hard to pull the weeds by hand and drag them to the dumpster. A slight feeling of doubt crept upon her as she continued her fight to remove those powerful weeds, so she sought confirmation from another guest who assured her those WERE weeds she was pulling out.

Sister Marietta came outdoors and asked Dante to come to her office. She shut the door and quietly informed her that she had pulled out her three-year prize: "Snow on the Mountains." To which Dante firmly replied that she had confirmed with several sources, and these snowy looking wonders were definitely weeds. She then went back outdoors and returned with one of her weeds in hand. Dante presented it to Sister who exclaimed, "My gosh, you were going to kill all of them!" And, as Dante described it, "Sister actually made a face at me."

Later that evening after having a good cry for all the wrong she had done to Sister, Dante put a single Snow on the Mountains in a vase and gave it to Sister saying, "I picked a flower for you."

– *Dante Clemens, Ex-guest*

CHAPTER 15

A Day in the Life

"Whatever you do for the least of my brothers and sisters, you do for me."

– MATTHEW 25:40

SISTER CAROL DIEMUNSCH, PUBLISHER OF CROSS CURRENTS, wrote the following account of a weekend spent at Emmaus House in 1991. Highlights from her story follow.

Rape. Sexual abuse. Drug addiction. Alcoholism. Homelessness. The streets. Prostitution. Jail. Experiences that we may have been spared, but not the women who come to Emmaus House.

At Emmaus, they find Sister Marietta Fritz and Sister Shirley Orand, who are ready to help, to listen, to love – 24 hours, every day. And, when the time comes to let go and say goodbye, the process begins again with another woman whom they welcome to Emmaus with assurances that she can get her life together.

SATURDAY, 2:30 P.M.

Patti is leaving today. She does not need much coaxing to tell her story: six months in jail for drug possession and separation from her husband who remains in jail. She has lost parental rights to her children. Today, however, she is smiling and singing as she packs her belongings and prepares to go to Bay City to start a new life, with a new job, and a reunion meeting with her children. "I am 35 now. It's time to wake up. I still have problems, but I can work them out."

SATURDAY, 4:25 P.M.

Sister Marietta phones a local bakery to see if they have leftover baked goods for distribution to the needy who live in this economically deprived area and who stop by Emmaus House for food. The news today is good: rolls, bread loaves, doughnuts, cookies, and coffee cakes. Sister comments, "We are in the poorest section of town. The people who live here live with the fear of being robbed, firebombed. And, so do we. But, we are here to be with the people we are serving."

SATURDAY, 7:00 P.M.

Gloria prepared dinner for us, very tasty barbecued ribs, then, quickly disappeared to her room, anxious to dress for the dance, an AA-sponsored event. She and Sister Shirley have carefully selected her attire from donated clothes. An hour later, she is nervously ready. "This is the first dance I have gone to in a long time when I wasn't loaded." It is agreed that tonight Sister Shirley will be waiting at 12:20 a.m. to welcome Gloria home from the dance. The Sisters are, indeed, surrogate parents.

SATURDAY, 7:30 P.M.

The house is quiet, with most of the guests out for the evening. This is a time for Shirley and Sister to sit down together and "catch up" on how each guest is doing, what repairs need to be made in the houses, how finances are shaping up, and so on. Often, it is late at night when they have the opportunity to talk or early in the morning, prior to the 8:00 a.m. morning meditation with the guests. Sister Marietta shares, "We are dealing with ladies from dope houses, houses of prostitution, the streets. In their addiction, they don't lead normal lives. We are just trying to let them see a different way of life – that God is good."

SUNDAY, 9:00 A.M.

Saturday night's discussion resumes. Sister Marietta concludes, "For the women here, success has different definitions. If they move forward on their path in life, even if they only stay for a week or two, at least, we've given them a taste. It may appear their prognosis is bleak, but there is a spark of the divine in each one of them. My goal is to ignite is so THEY can see it."

SUNDAY, 1:30 P.M.

Sister Shirley answers a phone call from Shaun, a former resident. She tells Sister that she is at the psychiatric hospital, soon to be discharged and requests to return to Emmaus. Sister goes to see her but reports upon her return that she is very concerned that Shaun will struggle with house rules. She is anorexic/bulimic and suicidal. At 21, she suffered cardiac arrest. If she does return, her behaviors, including eating habits will need to be carefully monitored.

SUNDAY, 5:00 P.M.

This weekend at Emmaus has been unusually calm; no former boyfriend or husband calling to demand money or begging a resident to return to him. None of the ladies threatened suicide or running; there were no emergency hospital trips.

Yet, there is always work, the work of listening to the guests' concerns and fears, the work to keep them focused on why they came to Emmaus, to rebuild their lives.

"We are called to somehow show these women that somebody still cares about them," concludes Sister Marietta. Sister Shirley adds, "We are called to just keep giving."

– Sister Carol Diemunsch

CHAPTER 16

Believing in Others

"And it shall come to pass, that whosoever shall call on the name of the Lord shall be saved."

– ACTS 2:21

SISTER MARIETTA FRITZ TAUGHT TO ALWAYS, WITHOUT EXCEPTION, BELIEVE IN OTHERS. Sister Marietta would often cite the best qualities of an individual who had fallen in some way. This core belief may be the key secret to the longevity and success of the Emmaus House of Saginaw.

One time a resident had violated a rule. It was the type of rule that, in Sister's eyes, was a non-negotiable and unforgiveable violation. The resident had violated the substance abuse rule, using a prohibited drug and endangering not only herself but also the lives of the others with whom she lived.

Thus, the resident had to leave.

In the process, Sister provided money for the resident to travel to another city, plus money for food. She said the woman needed a second chance, hoping she would listen to her advice to seek counseling upon her arrival to the new, out of town location. Sister criticized the decisions the resident had made, but not the person herself.

Subscribing to a belief that people can change, Sister delivered a type of "tough love" in cases where behavior ran counter to the culture she expected at the Emmaus House. Sister told me once that she felt the residents needed to accept the reality that Emmaus House was their one last chance. They needed to accept that and could not ignore rules and expectations. Residents of Emmaus House needed to show conformity and respect in return for trust from Sister and fellow residents.

An important part of these expectations was the commitment by Sister Marietta to provide safe and comfortable housing. "Each guest has her own place," Sister would proudly state. She knew first hand the experiences residents had had in jail or prison…group living quarters and no solitude.

Much noise exists in jails; I have visited the Saginaw County Jail and found it to be unbelievably loud and disconcerting. Others are similar.

Or worse!

Sister Marietta committed to a peaceful climate for each resident, believing in the power of redemption and the potential for each individual to change. By believing in others, Sister provided a path for change to occur. It was up to the individual to take the path.

– *Craig Douglas*

"I **love** the Lord,
for he heard my voice;

He heard my cry for mercy.
Because he turned his ear to me,
I will call on him as long as I live."

– PSALM 116:1-2

"**Start** where you are.
Use what you have.
Do what you can."

– ARTHUR ASHE (1943–93)

Me, opening Christmas gift
given to me by women here
(Diane by my side)

Freddie, Nellie, Stephanie, Sr. Mansell

"Bear with each other and *forgive* *one another,* *if any of you has a grievance* *against someone,* *forgive as the Lord forgave you."*

– COLOSSIANS 3:13

"Do not judge
and you will not be judged.
Do not condemn
and you will not be condemned.
Forgive, and you will be forgiven."

– LUKE 6:37

"Give thanks to the Lord
for he is good;
his love endures forever."

– PSALM 107:1

"When your *past* calls, don't answer. It has nothing new to say."

– FROM A COLLECTION
OF QUOTES BY HONDA KOTB,
THE NEW YORK TIMES

"Service to others
is the rent you pay
for your room here on earth."

– MUHAMMAD ALI (1942–2016)

"Those who *hope* in the Lord will *renew* their strength. They will *soar* on wings like eagles; they will *run* and not grow weary; they will *walk* and not faint."

– ISAIAH 40:31

"Remember
the days that you prayed
for the things you have now."

– (UNKNOWN)

"Have I not commanded you?
Be strong and courageous.
Do not be afraid;
do not be discouraged,
for the Lord your God
will be with you wherever you go."

– JOSHUA 1:9

CHAPTER 17

A Transformation

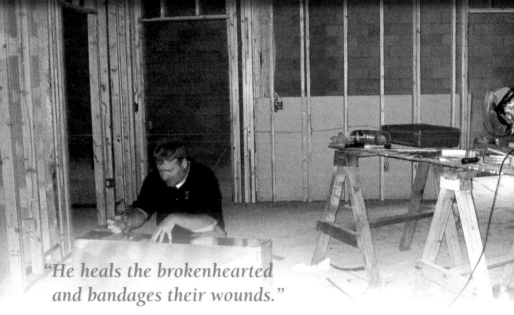

"He heals the brokenhearted and bandages their wounds."

— PSALM 147:2

"SISTER, SISTER, CAN WE FIX IT UP?" Rosalyn was ready to leave Emmaus House, but, in order for her to be reunited with her children, she needed a place of her own.

As Sister looked around the front room of this run-down house on Saginaw's east side, her silent thought was, "This place should be condemned." The rugs smelled, holes and mildew decorated every wall, and the front safety door did not close. Sister's reply to Rosalyn, however, was, "Sure we can fix it up, but it will take a lot of HARD work."

Two days later, they opened the door to a bedroom transformed by newly painted pastel walls (the result of mixing four buckets of leftover paint), a lovely mauve rug, fresh white curtains and blinds, a desk, a nightstand, even pictures to match the walls. Amazing! All items had been donated. This old room, through individuals sharing so much, had been healed. The transformation had begun.

It struck Sister that this is how all healing happens. Real healing is the cumulative collaborative effort of many people working together. Before this rehabbing job would be finished, more than 100 "helper healers" became involved.

Renovating Rosalyn's house taught Sister that God sculptures his helpers. She was not afraid to pick up a hammer and fix the door trim or use a utility knife to cut the rug. This project also taught Sister that all real healing is hard work. Although she admitted that her 52 year old back hurt for two days after all the bending over to cut that rug, the physical challenge of healing cannot compare with the challenge of healing a spirit and mind tortured by 10 or 20 years of abuse, neglect, and street living.

Sister explained that the guests of Emmaus fight these strenuous battles to gain wellness and healing; she believes they possess "the stuff of which saints are made." Sister recalls one "young saint", only 23, who had been hospitalized 18 times, suffered from bulimia/anorexia, was addicted to alcohol and drugs, and had attempted suicide several times. Her therapist explained that all of these problems were the result of brutal and consistent sexual abuse she had experienced since the age of 6. She has received support and therapy through Emmaus and has gone on to college, vowing that her healing will continue.

Sister speaks of her happiness for Rosalyn and her home, transformed. Even though the roof still leaks and some of the windows don't work right, there is a comfortable ambiance about the place. Sister believes that after healing has happened, we may believe we are healed, but we find that there are "spiritual leaky roofs" and "faith windows" which do not always work for us.

Healing is an ongoing process with no end time. We are all lifetime healers. And, as we strive to touch others and help them heal, we, too, are healed. As Sister reflects on her years at Emmaus, living with "thrown away" ladies, she is confident that this time in her life has given her the greatest time of healing – for her.

– *Joan Douglas*

CHAPTER 18

The Guests

"I press on...
because Christ Jesus has made me his own."

– PHILIPPIANS 3:12

Hello, my name is Rita. First of all, I would like to thank my God for a second chance, bringing me to Sister Marietta and Emmaus House. He knew it was the best answer, the best place for me to be. Living here at Emmaus House, with the patience of Sister and my new family, I am learning to grow, slowly, but surely. I now have hope, faith, and a willingness to keep trying. I'm renewed spiritually. I'm so grateful. Thank you, God, Sister, and the Emmaus House.

Hi, my name is Marcella. I am 31 years old, and I am truly grateful to be clean and sober and have Christ in my life today. I give God all the praise and glory for healing my mind, body, and spirit. I love the women I am discovering. I want to thank Sister Marietta for believing in me and giving me another chance. Because of her and some close friends, I still haven't stopped pushing. I'm a college student. I work part-time. I continue to build a relationship with Christ and most important, I work a 12-step program. I know that I still have a long way to go, but with God in my heart and mind, all things are possible. God bless.

Hello, my name is Jessica. I've been part of Emmaus House for about three years. How I ended up here is a blessing! I was only 18 years of age. Sister gave me an apartment to get a start in life. I knew about the program due to my mother staying here. Sadly, my parents couldn't give me the support that Sister has, which has been to take me to find a job, to get a job, and now to take me to work each day. Life used to be a struggle until my eyes were opened here. I am not addicted to anything, but for my family, it's a different story. So Sister took me in after I turned 18. Now, I can proudly say that God is good, and I am not alone. There are amazing programs for those willing. Life is too short to waste. I am thankful to be living yet another day.

Sister, I want you to know that I am truly grateful. I know that I am not always good at sharing or expressing it but I feel so blessed. I am so grateful you were here for me when I came out of prison, and I didn't have to feel alone. Thank you for your love and support and your advice and wisdom. I can never express how thankful I am for my new house. Thank you, Sister, for everything. You truly are an angel. *Brandy, Ex-guest*

Hi, my name is Katrina. I am currently a guest at Emmaus House for women re-entering society from prison, jail, or drug and alcohol rehab. I would like to encourage the women who are struggling with drugs and homelessness that there is help and hope. With the help of NA and the women of Emmaus House, I have been given a chance to spring back into life one day at a time! I am thankful to God for my new beginning.

Hi, my name is Shawne. I've been at Emmaus House over 18 months. I came here looking for direction. I wanted to start my life over again. Emmaus gave me that opportunity. I am currently enrolled at Delta College, getting grades not only that I am capable of, but grades I am proud of as well. I am blessed to have Sister Marietta and the Emmaus House staff in my life to remind me that the sky is the limit! Thank you.

Thank you. I could not have accomplished all that I have if I had not walked through the doors of Emmaus House. I thought I was trash before I came to Emmaus. Now, I feel like a contributing human being on this earth. Words can never say how much I thank you all. I could not have done this alone! Thank you with all my heart. *Lori, Ex-guest*

I'm thankful for my new home at Emmaus House. I've changed my life. I feel so good about myself, my spiritual awakening, and trying to do his will. I'm drug free, and will stay drug free! I pray to God that I can talk to my son, Jason, and he is reunited with my family.

The positive surroundings here have helped me and made me strong. I thank God for Sister Marietta and Ms. Southern and this program. Without this program I wouldn't be a free person today. I'm thankful for a second chance to get my life in order. So, I'm asking all to pray for me that I stay strong. I'm also asking God to bless me with some dentures, so I may smile again. My prayers are with you all. Thank you so much. *Christy V., Ex-guest*

Hi! My name is Beth. I arrived in Saginaw on a Greyhound bus on Sunday, March 28th, 2010. What little I owned I either wore or carried in a cardboard box. I was scared and alone. Sister Marietta had arranged for my roommate (House #8) to meet me at the bus station. What a relief! We immediately went to Emmaus House (House #1) where my AA "sponsor-by-mail" was waiting along with some residents and staff. How comforting to be among friends! My roommate, my sponsor, and I went over to the Morrow Center and picked out some clothes, shoes, purses, etc... We then grabbed a bite to eat and went home. My room was clean and tidy and welcoming. I settled in and slept.

Since then I've acclimated myself to the Emmaus House system – chores, meetings, groups, exercise classes, etc... I have a busy life orchestrated by God and Sister Marietta with lots of help from the rest of the staff and volunteers. I lack for nothing. All of this is possible because of the unfailing generosity of the donors who supply us with everything. Thank you all for sharing what you have. You've each contributed to the productive person I'm becoming. May God bless and keep you all! *Beth R., Ex-guest*

My name is Anne and I am 45 years old. I come from a small town up North; was married for 17 years, now divorced for the past eight years. I have two wonderful children ages 18 and 21. I have returned to the Emmaus House three different times. This last bit of sobriety has lasted five months. I would like to thank Sister and all the people who believe in me and are here to help me along my path to sobriety. It's a journey every day, and I love every minute of it. *Anne W., Ex-guest*

To the women here: Sometimes things don't work out the way you want them to. You feel as if the world is against you. It's not. Look how far you've come. Where would you really be if you didn't come to a safe place to start over, like Emmaus House. It's up to you how far you want to go. No one will take you by the hand, but just ask for help. The women here at Emmaus House will talk to you. Be real with yourself. Take the mask off. *Dorothy, Ex-guest*

(Note: Dorothy, 60, has spent almost half her adult life locked up. However, now she is in school to get her GED, took some refresher driving lessons, got her driver's license, participates in several self-improvement classes, has bought an old truck, and has joined the choir at her church. She's an inspiration to the younger women.)

Hi, my name is Joanne. I've been at the Emmaus House for one year and three months. I think the hardest part of recovery was to forgive myself for all of the bad things that I did in my addiction. Once I forgave myself and had faith in God everything started falling into place. I still have a long way to go in my recovery, and it's not an easy job. But, as long as I have God beside me everyday I know nothing bad can happen. Every day gets better and better. You just have to have faith! *Joanne P., Ex-guest*

My name is Jennifer. I came here to Emmaus House from Pittsburg. I'm a state parolee. I did seven years in the PA prison and I've got a long drug history. And, now, I have found peace in my life for the first time. Every day I'm here Sister teaches me something different about life, and when I lay my head down at night I feel safe, knowing that I made it through another day clean and sober. Thank God! *Jennifer., Ex-guest*

I lied, I cheated, I stole. I even sold my body. Life was about Lori. My days were planned around drinking and drugging. I hurt my family and close friends. I was the cause of many sleepless nights. I never got the chance to tell my mother I was sorry.

Today, with the help of Emmaus House, I have been sober for over a year. I am involved in 12-step groups. I attend Delta College. My kids actually like their mother and my grandbabies love me. I can't say enough about Emmaus House, the Sisters and volunteers. They have helped save another life, and for that, I will be ever grateful. Thank you. *Lori Y., Ex-guest*

Hi, my name is Kris, and I have been at Emmaus House for three years. Sister Marietta and Sister Mary Elizabeth have been very good to me. I am a very blessed woman since I've been clean and sober. I have been going to college part time and holding down a job for the past three years. Now, I will be starting a second job on August 26th. So whoever is feeling depressed and thinking bad, just stay clean and keep your faith. Prayers work. I just recently moved out on my own. Now I have the responsibilities that I didn't have before, and I'll take the time to succeed. God has turned my life around. Amen. Kris M., Ex-guest

ADDICTION

Too scared to face emotions kept inside
fear that what I have survived I can still die.
Push it back to ignore the pain
choose a drug to numb my brain.
Addiction takes over control
I begin to bury my soul.
I've fallen so deep this drug now consumes me
no memory left of what or who I used to be.
This drug has taken over I can't believe my eyes
my body is gone to the years that went by.
So disgusted with how I feel
too hard to face it and feel everything.
Addiction is no longer a friend
I want to live again
I will no longer pray for my own death
I want to live until God gives my last breath.

Elizabeth S., Ex-guest

CHAPTER 19

"Love"

"A time to love, and a time to hate;
a time of war, and a time of peace."

– ECCLESIASTES 3:8

SISTER MARIETTA FRITZ IS A PERSON WHO LOVES AND IS A PERSON WHO IS LOVED. *Unconditionally.*

I cannot recall the day that it dawned on me that Joan and I love Sister. It was an evolving understanding by both of us; Sister Marietta is a person we love.

The origin was when we started volunteering back in July 2013. We would arrive at 8:30 a.m. and begin a three hour adventure. Joan would drive the ladies to their appointments; I would tag along with Bill Schaefer to assist with repairs. In these roles we would weave in-and-out of situations and in many of them Sister Marietta was front and center. We would reflect afterwards in a sort of "debriefing" and often marvel at how well Sister had helped someone with a problem.

In January, 2014, Joan and I arrived after a period of extreme snowfall. I am sure there was five inches blanketing the parking lot, but looking back, it seems as if it was more like a foot. Nevertheless, it was nearly impossible to navigate the lot, and moneys to hire a plow were not in the plan. So, I volunteered to shovel.

Sister was puzzled at first to think I would manually shovel the parking lot. She said things like, "It is awfully cold out there." A few comments of "be careful" were thrown in; it was her effort to assure me that it did not have to be done.

I don't recall why Bill Schaefer was not there that day, but he wasn't, and it freed me up to do the task. So, I started shoveling, one parking space at a time. Many times, I had to shovel around parked cars that had been hopelessly snowed in. While it was not pretty, the lot soon became more tolerable, and I felt a sense of accomplishment in taking on the challenge.

After about an hour, Sister was worried about me. She sent Joan out to check on me, and, during one break when I went inside, she was pretty direct in suggesting that I stop. I could feel her love and concern for my well-being. It was certainly appreciated, and in our "debrief", both Joan and I concluded that Sister loved both of us.

When Sister Marietta fell in the summer of 2015, she suffered a broken knee and was in a wheel chair for quite a while. The outpouring of love and support for her was tremendous; it was a clear reflection of the affection others have for her.

– *Craig Douglas*

CHAPTER 20

A New Role

"That is why, for Christ's sake,
I delight in weaknesses, in insults, in hardships,
in persecutions, in difficulties.
For when I am weak, then I am strong."

— CORINTHIANS II, 12:10

I NEVER DREAMED I WOULD BE SITTING AT SISTER MARIETTA'S DESK in an official capacity. There I was, however, acting as the Interim Executive Director. It still seems a rather surreal period in my life.

The former Director had departed, and, with her, the Social Worker/Case Manager and our volunteer for financial matters. Since I was a member of the Board of Directors and a volunteer at Emmaus,

I was more familiar with the day to day activities and responsibilities, and so I was voted "into office."

Thankfully, Sister Mary Elizabeth stepped up from her five hours on Friday afternoon shift, and, when she was not teaching religion in the elementary school, she came to Emmaus and handled financial matters, correspondence, donations, and she helped me to maintain my focus – keep the organization running as smoothly as we are able. She was and is my safety net.

The challenges quickly mounted. After four days of dealing with guests' needs, frustrations (they desperately fear change) and worries

for the future of Emmaus, one of our guests used illegal substances. It was on a Saturday. I was out of town. The House Manager, Donna, worked with her, stayed with her through the night, and I was called on Sunday. Although the rule broken meant dismissal, I knew she had nowhere to go on a moment's notice, so, with strict sanctions put in place for the next 30 days, including not leaving the Emmaus campus and intensive counseling, she remained with us.

Tammy had good days and bad when depression overwhelmed her. She continued to thank me for a second chance, but other guests thought I had acted with too much leniency, resented her presence and let me know their feelings quite forcefully. I was reminded of what Sister Marietta had once shared with me, "There is never the luxury of focusing all of one's attention on solving just one problem." Bills must be paid; the week's schedule must be planned; phone calls returned, and new guests arrive. I would have given anything to see Sister standing in the office doorway, ready to help me deal with the pressures I was feeling.

As the second week progressed, we were notified that a 2-day HUD review was coming up. Our Shelter Plus Care clients' files would be reviewed, and they would interview at least two clients in their homes and do inspections. I had no idea what our responsibilities entailed with these clients who had "graduated" from the program, living on their own, with the exception of Barbara who was a volunteer. Amy Bartels Roe, a dear friend, who is the Executive Director of The Mustard Seed, another non-profit agency, also involved in this review, helped us navigate through the process. And, of course, the other day to day issues and conflicts did not go away.

As the third week unfolded, Donna, the House Manager, and truly my right hand, asked me if I planned to attend Drug Court. Four of our guests were in this program. The purpose of this Court was to prevent the offenders from time in jail if they followed a strict set of rules for behavior, counseling, random drug testing, and maintaining a notebook detailing their progress and the activities and meetings in which they were involved. Thus, Monday became my busiest day.

Dispensing weekly medications for the guests was my morning responsibility. Given that all guests remembered to bring their medication panels with them, I could complete the task in about 2 1/2 hours; with interruptions and phone calls, sometimes longer. I left for Drug Court at 3:10 p.m.; it convened from 3:30–5:30 p.m. Drug Court gave me a much deeper knowledge of the drug use problem in our community. The majority of the offenders were young, under 30. Their stories told before the judge were both, very sad, but, in most situations, hopeful. Although they had faced arrests, loss of jobs, homes, and children, they were now being given the tools to make changes in their lives. Judge Boes asked questions which caused them to reflect upon how they were living, managing their time, and what productive things they were doing to find jobs, continue their education, and build relationships, especially with their families. If they had missed a curfew or had "used" a substance, because they are under such strict regulations, Judge Boes already knew, and they knew a consequence for their behavior would result.

After several weeks of sitting through the sometimes, painful question and answer sessions, I was struck by the success stories. Eutevia was nearly finished with her GED program she was working hard to complete. Kristy was moving into her own apartment and holding down two part-time jobs. Jackie had gained partial custody of her two girls, three days weekly. I realized without this program of accountability and a Judge who cared about them, their progress toward their goals may never have occurred. I determined I would return in the future, after my Interim service was done, to observe and listen and know we do have a system in place which operates on the premise that anyone who desires help, can be helped.

– Joan Douglas

CHAPTER 21

Taking the Reigns

*"She opens her mouth with wisdom,
and the teaching of kindness is on her tongue."*

— PROVERBS 31:26

IN THE FIRST DAYS OF MY NEW ASSIGNMENT, I did not have a plan, a priority list, or an outline of steps to take to keep this organization moving forward, but I had Sister Mary Elizabeth by my side, and that was enough.

Some kind of common sense took over, in that, we opened mail, paid bills, listened to voice messages, and listened to our guests and our employees. Sister would come to Emmaus House during her lunch break and again after her school day ended at 3:30. She often stayed well into the evening hours. My respect for her ability to teach children all day and wedge in several more hours at Emmaus House deepened.

Sister's math background and bookkeeping skills were vitally important in keeping day to day operations on track. Her support for me in my decision making kept me on track.

I recall the day Sister came back from the bank after working through the tasks of changing signatures on accounts and sorting out the many details involved in this transition. She walked into the office and quietly said, "Well, I cried today." There were those days when the responsibilities facing us seemed unending. I think that I cried that day, also, as I drove home, feeling inadequate and wanting so badly to call Sister Marietta and cry "Help!!"

More than anything, I knew our guests needed to know that we would not jump ship, but would remain with them, helping them in their recovery and formulating a plan, ultimately, to find the right and permanent leadership for Emmaus House.

– *Joan Douglas*

CHAPTER 22

A Time to Perform

"I do not pray for success; I pray for faithfulness."

– MOTHER THERESA

IN THAT FIRST WEEK AT EMMAUS, I was quickly made aware of prior commitments which I needed to address. Speaking engagements, in the short run, needed to be postponed with our thanks and plans to reschedule when permanent leadership was in place. And, then, at the YMCA, I looked up and saw Renee Johnston, CEO and President of the Saginaw Community Foundation, walking quickly toward me with a question, "The Emmaus ladies are still planning to perform for the Foundation's event, aren't they? I hope they won't cancel!"

Frankly, either "cancel" or "postpone" was going to be my response, but I quickly decided to take a leap of faith and confirm the performance.

When I arrived at Emmaus that same morning, I asked our House Manager, Donna, if she knew whether the guests had begun rehearsing for the Foundation event; they had not. Recalling that they had performed "Amazing Grace" at the February concert fundraiser, I thought we could revive that, at least. However, only three of our guests were still with us, so we did not have much experience on our

side. Our Sheriff, William Federspiel, had graciously accompanied the ladies, so I contacted him, requesting his help again; he accepted. I then turned to a friend, Jill Vary, choir member from our church and a member of the Saginaw Choral Society, and asked her to direct us in this adventure. We had about 2 1/2 weeks to learn the music. We added "Just A Closer Walk With Thee" and began rehearsing.

Other than our "Three Musketeers," none of the ladies had sung in public before. Our group lacked confidence. But, Jill was willing and enthusiastic, and so it went. The ladies starting out, hoping to hit the right notes, but frequently stopping and staring at Jill and repeating, "We sound terrible." We kept working.

Some excitement was generated when Virginia, the residential assistant, located the concert outfits from February's performance – white, dressy, blouses and long black skirts. Incredibly, everyone found an outfit that fit, and they began to feel more like a group, a choir. Unfortunately, we were under rehearsed to no one's fault; we had little time, busy schedules, and other obligations going on. My role was to be the convincing, encouraging cheerleader. I did my best.

Show time...we arrived early and watched the crowd grow. This was an outdoor event to celebrate and thank those who donate to the Community Foundation. Questions from our ladies began... "Why didn't you tell us there would be so many people?" "Is it ok if I just move my mouth?" The question I could answer much to their happiness and relief was, "Yes, you may eat from the buffet." And, so, Jill bravely directed them through "Just A Closer Walk" and "Amazing Grace." We survived.

After the applause and the "thank-you's" had ended and the very good food consumed, it all seemed a rewarding endeavor. One of the guests leaned over toward me and said quietly, "I'm sorry we were so awful, Miss Joan." We had kept our obligation, and the community was aware that, even though major change was occurring at Emmaus House, the beat must go on, ...must go on, and, indeed, it was.

– Joan Douglas

CHAPTER 23

Enter Donna

*"It is such a comfort to drop the tangles of life
into God's hands and leave them there."*

— LETTIE COWMAN

DONNA CAME TO EMMAUS HOUSE AS A GUEST and quickly demonstrated her determination to make permanent changes in her life, her recovery. She is a leader, a former teacher, a person who really did know what the ladies go through as they work to rebuild their lives.

When I was serving as Interim Director, Donna served as the House 1 Manager, the Emmaus House "headquarters." With Sister Elizabeth's blessing and the reminder that Sister Marietta had hired an assistant to help her, we named Donna to the position of Assistant Executive Director. It was a significant step in rebuilding Sr. Marietta's program.

We returned to the process of seeking candidates for the Executive Director's position. We held interviews. We had a strong candidate but could not negotiate a salary. Time passed. I do not recall at what point I decided to pray daily for direction, that the face I saw in front of me was Donna's. I decided it was time to take my recommendation to the Emmaus Board of Directors.

While all of the board members had met Donna, I brought her to the next board meeting to more formally introduce her and to give them the opportunity to ask questions. At the end of the regular session, we adjourned into closed session and unanimously voted to appoint Donna our new Executive Director.

– *Joan Douglas*

CHAPTER 24

Donna's Story

"For I know the plans I have for you
declares the Lord, plans for welfare
and not for evil, to give you a future and a hope."

– JEREMIAH 29:11

"HOW WAS I TO KNOW THAT THIS PLACE CALLED THE EMMAUS HOUSE WOULD SAVE MY LIFE? That it would be a place to heal the wounds of addiction, a place to repair all of the wreckage of my past.

I came here in July of 2017 from a treatment facility in Macomb County. I was broken, frail, and hopeless. This was one of the many attempts I had made in the past to change my life. I had no idea at the time what this place would hold in store for me. I finally had both the opportunity and a safe place to recover and learn a better way of life. One of the many attributes which was most instrumental in my stay was that I could stay as long as I needed to. Recovery from addiction does not have a deadline; it doesn't work that way. It is so important that we do not impose a time limit upon our guests.

I became a House 1 Manager in February of 2018. When I was promoted to Assistant Director, I realized I had found my purpose in this new life I had created. I became Executive Director in June 2019, and I have come to realize the amazing blessings of helping women move forward out of addiction and homelessness, into a life of independence and success. I watch the women reunite with their children and loved ones and watch the confidence build inside them as they rebuild their lives.

I now move forward to meet the challenge and responsibility to keep the Emmaus House operating and continuing to save lives. Although it is challenging, I have the confidence and ability today, thanks to this organization, to maintain and build this very necessary program."

– *Donna Clarke*

CHAPTER 25

Takila's Story

"Brothers, I do not consider that I have made it on my own. But, one thing I do: forgetting what lies behind and straining forward to what lies ahead."

– PHILIPPIANS 3:13

ON THE DAY THAT TAKILA ARRIVED AT EMMAUS HOUSE, I was the Interim Executive Director as well as the person who conducted the intake process. I saw a sad, quiet woman, who, when she attempted to describe any part of her life which brought her to us, was interrupted by tears. Takila struggled to regain composure in order to answer the questions I needed to ask. I took time. I repeated questions for clarification. I found I was fighting back my tears as her story unfolded – living in the streets, facing abandonment, jail, back to the streets, again and again.

We somehow made it through the process. I said a few words of encouragement. I paused, allowing time for her to collect her thoughts. I asked if she had any questions for me. Takila paused, looked straight at me and asked, "Do you know where I can get a haircut?" A bond of friendship had formed.

I asked Takila to share a bit about her background, and here is what she shared: "Emmaus House has allowed me to become the responsible individual that I always knew I could be. I have accomplished a lot of short-term goals while here; I recently obtained my driver's license. I am a House Manager, and I am able to maintain my sobriety."

I had not worked in over twenty years but since coming to Emmaus House, I have maintained employment. I have been encouraged when I was down, encouraged to face my fears, and encouraged to be a better person, always caring for others.

I am truly blessed to be a part of Emmaus; it's a place where you can really take the time to know who you are. I really enjoy being a part of this journey. I have learned to live again.

Sometimes, life's lessons are not easy, but I know I have support all around me when things get rough. I would also like to thank Sister Marietta for starting this program to help women like me get back into the mainstream of life. At one time, I had no hope because I was living a life with no meaning; today, I am hopeful that my life will always have meaning."

– Joan Douglas, with help from Takila
in her own words about "her story"

CHAPTER 26

Saginaw Leaders' Perspectives

by AMY BARTELS ROE

Executive Director – Mustard Seed Shelter

It was in 1987 that my parents were working on a project with our local court system. Through one of our Saginaw County judges, they had the pleasure of hearing about and consequently meeting both Sr. Marietta and Sr. Shirley.

My parents immediately began helping out with this ministry in any way they could and as I was at a perfect age to pitch in myself, I was often in tow with them as we went to volunteer at Emmaus House.

I was also at a perfect age, 12 years, to be open to truly seeing and feeling God's presence at Emmaus House, led by Sr. Marietta. I witnessed and was able to shadow a true servant of God – an experience that I will never forget and that has played an important role in having shaped me into the servant of our Lord that I strive to be each and every day.

A listener, a mother, a friend, a coordinator, a person who exercises tough-love and sets boundaries, a beautiful person of faith. This is who I met when I met Sr. Marietta Fritz, and there is no doubt that this is the case for all whom she has met.

I actively volunteered at Emmaus House until the time I was off to college and had the pleasure in high school of working with Sister and a team of others in starting an after-school drop in program in the church building across the parking lot from Houses 1 and 2. It was a blessing to have her (along with other adults), lead a group of teenagers through the process of what was needed to create such an opportunity for the kids in the neighborhood and so many children found safety there.

As an adult, our paths began to cross again as I began my career working with the poor. We sat in meetings together and it was an amazing feeling to add yet another description of her – colleague.

One funny story: During a time just about seven years ago, Marietta and I went for a drive as I was interested in seeing all of the, then 14 houses that were part of Emmaus.

As we were driving, one of the Emmaus guests called my cell phone and asked to speak with Sister. The guest wanted to know where something was in Sister's office. Now, if you ever had the chance of visiting her office, you will know what I am talking about. Sister explained to the guest that she just needed to sit in the chair at her desk, pull the chair in close, put out her right hand with a slight bend in her elbow and drop it down to locate the item she was looking for

– and it worked – on first try! She knew exactly where everything was no matter how "messy" it may have seemed.

I liken this to her ministry…no matter how messy or broken someone is and may seem, Marietta knows exactly how to find them and lead them to a better way of life, a home. through the grace of God.

VERONICA HORN
President/CEO – Saginaw County Chamber of Commerce
I was just amazed when I met Sr. Marietta through the Christian Service Commission. I learned about her Ministry at the Saginaw County Jail and how she and Sr. Shirley had this idea to rehabilitate the women who were being released.

They KNEW that they could teach, by example, how women could learn the basic skills to get their children back from foster care, how they could learn, by example, to dress for a job interview. The only requirement was that the person had to go to a Church Service once a week. Any church service.

The program was so wildly successful that word got out and Sr. Marietta was contacted by an agency of the federal government, telling her that they wanted to use her model and could fund her

program. The only stipulation was that they had to take the "religious" artifacts; read in crucifixes down and they couldn't require the women to attend a church service.

Sr. Marietta explained in her wonderful way that these were a big part of the reason the Emmaus House WAS successful. She refused the money and said (in so many words) "God will Provide."

Well, God certainly has; through so many in the community that believe in this ministry and have given time, talent and treasures to the Emmaus House. Sr. Marietta and Sr. Shirley were/are truly gifts from God.

PAUL C. CHAFFEE LLC
Executive Communications Consultation

My first encounter with the Notorious Sister Marietta was early a winter morning at a meeting of the Community Affairs Committee, more commonly known as the "bishop's breakfast."

The mostly revered (in some quarters not-so-revered), Bishop Kenneth Untener founded the group in the late '80s. It's a group of community leaders like none others in Saginaw County. I like to

think of it as the audience you'd most like not to screw up in front of university presidents, politicians, agency heads, government leaders, captains of industry and commerce.

The format emphasizes time for these leaders to get to know each other and perhaps develop trust and familiarity. That way in the event of a community disaster or extraordinary opportunity, the founding bishop supposed, the organizations they lead would more likely cooperate based on their personal familiarity. Question time follows locally topical presentations.

NSM was there to talk about Emmaus House, relatively freshly launched at that time.

This diminutive lady's explanation of her project was so passionate, so persuasive, so simply direct that she locked in the focus of everyone listening.

I've attended these meetings for four decades and, honestly, if you asked me to I probably couldn't recall more than a couple dozen of the topics. And that includes my own times at the podium. Hers is as fresh in mind as though it were last week.

She gained supporters, including me, whose backing for Emmaus house that still exists. One does not say no to her humble requests.

Sister Marietta's energy so saturates the Emmaus House fiber that it has continued well after her retirement. Bless you NSM and the work you so nobly have started.

SISTER MARY ELIZABETH KLIER

I knew Sr. Marietta for a couple of years before I came to work at Emmaus House in 2000. When Sr. Marietta learned that I was leaving my previous work in June of 2000, she offered me a job to come and help her at Emmaus House.

In 2000, Emmaus House had only four houses. During Sr. Marietta's time at Emmaus House, we grew to 14 houses and were able to have 50 women live in our various homes.

Looking back on that time, I wonder how we were able to have all those homes and the 50 women that we had living with us for a time.

Somehow, by the grace and help of God, it happened and worked well. Sr. Marietta knew each woman and was able to somehow take time for each one.

Before a possible future director came to Emmaus House, I worked very closely in the same office with Sr. Marietta. Our two desks were in that "small" space where our present director works. I was able to witness and experience her interactions with the women. Sometimes, and maybe, many times, Sister gave them "tough" love, but they came out better for it.

I'm very thankful for all those many years that I had learning from and working with Sr. Marietta!

EPILOGUE

"Our faith can move mountains."

— MATTHEW 17:20

SISTER MARIETTA OFTEN SAID, "LIFE IS NOT FOR THE FAINT OF HEART." NOR, IS LIFE AT EMMAUS HOUSE. THE WORK OF CHANGING LIVES AND LIVING IN RECOVERY IS A DAILY CHALLENGE FOR OUR GUESTS AND FOR THOSE WHO GUIDE THEM.

Donna Clarke and Jen Hauch, our current Executive Director and Assistant Director, have accepted this challenge to lead, to support, to pick up the pieces when needed and to keep going. We have sad days when a guest loses her battle and returns to the streets. We have heartbreaking days when the call comes announcing an ex-guest's death to overdose or violence.

The key to all of this lies in sharing the burdens and the joys. We celebrate when another guest "graduates" from Drug Court. We celebrate when children want to spend time with their mothers. We celebrate when GED's are completed, when employment becomes possible. We celebrate when we see a guest take the time to listen to another's struggles and be that solid rock so desperately needed.

We rejoice that in over 33 years, we have been able to provide homes for women in need, we have paid the bills, and as Sister would say, "We have kept the lights on."

May the light of Emmaus House burn brightly for a very long time, a symbol of hope, of victory through our Lord and Savior.

Amen.

— Joan Douglas

SISTER MARIETTA

✠

SAGINAW'S SAINT

Joan & Craig Douglas – Authors

Thank you for reading our book about Sr. Marietta Fritz and Emmaus House.

**WE INVITE YOU TO BECOME
A "FRIEND OF EMMAUS HOUSE."**
*There are levels of annual support from which
you may choose that defrays operational costs
or earmarked as requested by the donor:*

STANDARD	
Individual	$ 50
Business / Organization	200

BRONZE	
Individual	$ 100
Business / Organization	500

SILVER	
Individual	$ 500
Business / Organization	1000

GOLD	
Individual	$ 1000 or more
Business / Organization	5000 or more

Checks payable to: Emmaus House of Saginaw
Indicate on check: Friends
Mail to: Emmaus House of Saginaw
    733 S. 14th Street
    Saginaw, Michigan 48601

Visit: www.emmaushousesaginaw.com
Select: Donations

"Thank you so very much for your support."

*"The two were going to a village named Emmaus...
and Jesus drew near and walked along with them."*

– LUKE 24: 13-15